Crime

Judith Anderson

amicus

Published by Amicus
P.O. Box 1329, Mankato, Minnesota 56002

Printed in the United States of America at Corporate Graphics, in North Mankato, Minnesota.

Published by arrangement with the Watts Publishing Group Ltd., London.

Library of Congress Cataloging-in-Publication Data

Anderson, Judith.
  Crime / by Judith Anderson.
      p. cm. -- (Media power)
  Summary: "Discusses the media treatment of crime worldwide, including issues
of media pressure, privacy, discrimination, and scandals"--Provided by publisher.
  Includes bibliographical references and index.
  ISBN 978-1-60753-113-5 (library binding)
  1. Crime in mass media--Juvenile literature. 2. Mass media and crime--Juvenile literature.
  3. Crime and the press--Juvenile literature. I. Title.
  P96.C74A53 2011
  364.2'54--dc22

                                                              2009051452

Series editor: Julia Bird
Design: Nimbus Design

Picture credits:
Aberystwyth/Alamy: 38; John Birdsall/PAI: 15, 36; Mike Booth/Alamy: 18;
CBS/Everett/Rex Features: 40; Caroline Contino/BEI/Rex Features: 27;
David Fisher/Rex Features: 32; John Giles/PA Archive/PAI: 33; Garry He/AP/PAI: 19.
Jeremy Horner/Corbis: 34; Hulton-Deutsch/Corbis: 8; Lenny Iguelz/AP/PAI: 10,
Image Source/Rex Features: 11; Nils Jorgensen/Rex Features: 41.
KPA/Zuma/Rex Features: 9; Dominic Lipinski/PAI: 12; Ilene MacDonald/Alamy: 13.
Rick Maiman/Sygma/Corbis: 17; Toby Melville/Corbis: 24; Murray/Rex Features: 22.
Tracey Nearmy/epa/Corbis: 21; PA Archive/PAI: 14; Chris Radburn/PA Archive/ PAI: 26;
Rex Features: 29, 37; Laura Segall/NY Times/Reducx Pictures/Eyevine: 28;
Alex Segre/Alamy: 39; Sipa Press/Rex Features: 25, 31; Ted Soqui/Corbis: 23.
Steve Starr/Corbis: 16; STR/epa/Corbis: 30; Jean-Michel Turpin/Corbis: 20.
Danny Young/Rex Features: 35.

1212
32010

9 8 7 6 5 4 3 2 1

Contents

Crime:
A Public Interest

Crime concerns us all. We want to feel safe and finding out about crime helps us to protect ourselves against it. We are curious, too, about things that we hope will never happen to us. Fortunately, most people don't experience crime on a regular basis. So we look to the media to tell us about it.

Case Study: The Impact of Television

The spread of television in the mid-twentieth century brought serious crime into people's living rooms for the first time. This was highlighted by the murders of five children in northern England in the mid-1960s. Television crews followed the police as they searched the open countryside for bodies in a case the media dubbed the Moors murders. When Ian Brady and Myra Hindley were convicted of the murders, their photographs appeared on news bulletins around the world. Television audiences followed the case and its horrifying details. Because of the intense media coverage they received, the Moors murders have not been forgotten. They have also been blamed for the increasing fear about children's safety that is still with us today.

This photograph of Moors murderer Myra Hindley has been reproduced so often that it is one of the most famous images of the 1960s.

The Media's Response

Editors and producers respond to this demand for information. TV news programs, documentaries, films, newspapers, and the radio cover stories about the bad things that people do. Sometimes, the most shocking or extreme crimes are the ones we want to know about most. And the media thrives on giving us what we want.

A False Impression?

The crimes that receive the most attention in the media are not usually the most common ones. Most people are far more interested in a serious crime such as murder than in common crimes such as vandalism or theft. Murder is very rare in most neighborhoods, but the media coverage that it receives can create the impression that it is far more widespread.

• Up for Discussion •

The Australian TV program, *Crime Investigation Australia*, reconstructs gruesome murders. Many other TV channels around the world broadcast real-life crimes. Why do you think these programs choose to focus on murder and violence?

What type of crime concerns you most?

The 1996 murder of child beauty queen JonBenet Ramsey in Colorado received intense media coverage. Her attacker has never been caught, though journalists have speculated at length about who killed her.

What's New?

Every year seems to bring a new crime wave. Dramatic headlines help to focus our attention on the latest fear: knife or gun crime, car jacking, drug crime, and illegal immigration. We want to know what's new and what's changing—and the media wants to keep us interested.

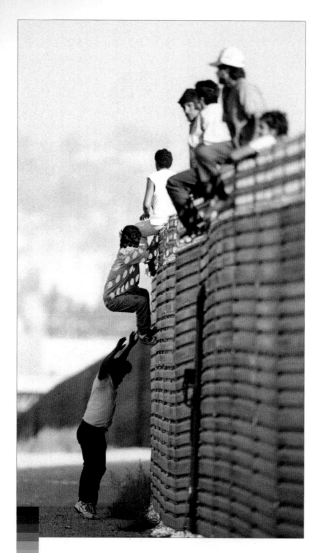

Crimes such as illegal immigration have been around for a long time, but pictures such as this can create the impression that they are a new threat.

New Threats

The media reflects public opinion, but it also informs people about new threats. When this is done responsibly, it provides a vital public service in the fight against crime. Twenty years ago, there was no Internet crime, because there was no Internet. Now people are much more aware of the need to protect themselves against identity theft and online fraud because of the way these issues have been highlighted in the media.

Changing Attitudes

Of course, crime has always existed. Yet public attitudes toward different types of behavior change over time. Our laws about drugs, sex, violence in the home, racial prejudice, and homophobia have all undergone transformations in the past 100 years. In the nineteenth century, author Oscar Wilde was imprisoned for practicing homosexuality after a trial that was sensationalized by the media. However, race discrimination was

Case Study: Hoodies

Over the last few years, young people who wear hoodies—hooded tops—have become associated with a perceived rise in antisocial behavior. This is because a hoodie can obscure the wearer's face, preventing identification by CCTV cameras or members of the public. As a result, hooded tops have been banned from many U.S. schools and even some shopping centers in the United Kingdom—whether or not the wearer is behaving suspiciously. The word "hoodie" has become a form of media shorthand used in news headlines to express a public fear of young people. However, many hoodie-wearers argue that this is an unfair stereotype that ignores the real issues and statistics about crime.

• Up for Discussion •

What types of crime do you think are on the increase? Why?

Some argue that headlines such as "Hoodie thugs" increase our fear of crime. Others say that the media simply reflects public opinion about crime. What do you think?

not a crime and was not reported. Today, many countries have laws to protect people from different forms of prejudice, and the media tends to reflect our changing attitudes.

Are hoodie-wearers more likely to be criminals, or is this a media stereotype?

Fighting Crime

The police, government, and other anticrime campaigners frequently use the media to help fight crime. Sometimes they advertise in newspapers and on TV or make appearances on TV or radio to get their message across. Often they set up a press conference to highlight a crime story and attract media attention.

The Press Conference

The police will call a press conference when they want to put out an appeal for information or witnesses or to put pressure on offenders and their families to come forward. The media are invited to ask questions, take photographs, reproduce CCTV images, and convey the police's version of events. They might also be asked to publicize a telephone hotline or a web site set up to deal with a particular case. Most media organizations are very willing to take part. The police get the publicity they want, and the media get a news story. Sometimes, however, the police will request a news blackout from the media, particularly if the crime involves hostages or kidnap victims.

A British woman, Lindsay Hawker, was murdered in Japan in 2007. Her family gave press conferences to appeal for help in finding her killer.

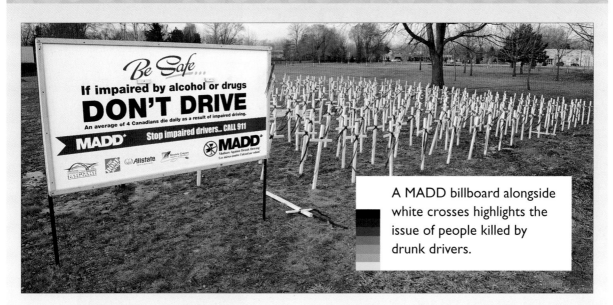

A MADD billboard alongside white crosses highlights the issue of people killed by drunk drivers.

Every year, the police and other campaigners, such as MADD (Mothers Against Drunk Driving), use the media to tackle the crime of drunk driving. Catchy titles such as "Highways or dieways?" and "Sober or slammer?" are used in their campaigns. Press conferences in hospitals highlight the dangers. A 2008 social awareness campaign in Canada used a series of web-based videos known as "Paul's Story." The videos told the story of a fictional teenager, Paul, coping with the consequences of killing and injuring his friends after drinking and driving. Facebook pages and blogs were used to extend the campaign.

New Media

The police are increasingly turning to video-sharing Internet sites such as YouTube to place appeals for information, CCTV footage of suspects, and short films about the dangers of drugs or carrying weapons. These sites are seen as important tools by some campaigners. Not only are they more likely to reach a young audience, but they can appear amateurish or homemade, which appeals to those who might distrust or ignore an official message.

• *Up for Discussion* •

Some anticrime campaigns emphasize the consequences for the victims of crime— such as death, injury, and trauma. Other campaigns focus on the consequences for the perpetrators—prison, fines, and public disgrace. Which type of campaign do you think is most effective? Why?

Your Call Counts!

Some TV shows are made with the help of the police. They aim to discover new leads for unsolved crimes by encouraging viewers to call in with information. Shows such as *America's Most Wanted* and *Crimewatch* broadcast interviews with witnesses, reenactments of crimes, and CCTV footage in order to jog people's memories.

A Public Service

The producers of these shows say that they are performing a public service with a good success rate in terms of convictions. Members of the public may call anonymously, and all new information is examined carefully by the police. The programs do not usually offer a reward. However, the success of the show depends on the size of the audience. The more people who watch, the better the level of response. Some people think that the pressure to attract large audiences may distort the way some crimes are presented.

Featured Crimes

Which crimes do the programs feature? Producers of Britain's *Crimewatch* have said that the police must be able to present a new angle or lead for a case to be broadcast. And, of course, crimes are more interesting if the program contains visual evidence or reenactments. Tragically, *Crimewatch* host Jill Dando was murdered by an unknown assailant in 1999. The show that featured a reconstruction of her murder was one of the most watched in the history of the series.

Crimewatch host Jill Dando was murdered in 1999. Her killer has never been caught.

Case Study: Crime Stoppers

Crime Stoppers is a not-for-profit community organization that works with the local police and media to solve crimes.

Crime Stoppers began in Albuquerque, New Mexico, in 1976 when police Detective Greg MacAleese reached a dead end in a murder investigation. Frustrated by the lack of clues, he turned to the media and persuaded a local television station to produce a reenactment of the crime. Within 72 hours of the reenactment being aired, the police received a tip that helped solve the murder.

The Crime Stoppers concept is now widespread in many countries, including the United States, United Kingdom, Canada, and Australia. The public can call a hotline anonymously and leave information. If this leads to an arrest, the informant can claim a cash reward—if they request one. The informant is given a code number so that their identity stays secret.

A Crime Stoppers billboard in the United States offers anonymity and a cash reward in exchange for information.

• Up for Discussion •

Many TV programs such as *America's Most Wanted* show detailed reconstructions of crimes. Do you think people watch them for information or entertainment? Does it matter?

The Thrill
of the Chase

The success of any media outlet depends on the size of its audience. TV programs, web sites, and newspapers compete against each other for a share of that audience. So how can a media outlet gain an advantage over its rivals?

A Dangerous Pursuit

Many news organizations seek to improve their audience ratings by being the first to break the news, being closest to the action, and providing the most dramatic coverage of events as they unfold. Some news networks dispatch helicopters to follow police response vehicles when a crime is committed. They hope to film the action from above. Car chases are particularly popular as they can be followed from the air and generally result in arrests on the ground after some spectacularly dangerous driving. However, several TV crews may end up following the same car. In 2007, four people were killed in Arizona when two helicopters from rival networks collided in midair.

Police, Camera, Action!

A number of TV shows rely on video footage of car chases supplied to them by the police, usually for a fee. When this occurs, the police usually point out that the fees are spent on road safety improvements and these programs help

Helicopters carrying TV crews can transmit live coverage to audiences to view the action.

• Up for Discussion •

Do programs showing high-speed police car chases encourage dangerous driving or do they provide a public service? Why are they so popular?

to educate the public by showing the consequences of criminal behavior when suspects are caught and arrested.

However, some people argue that the presence of cameras simply encourages the police to initiate more chases, making criminals attempt bigger stunts that seriously endanger innocent pedestrians and other vehicles and passengers. Dangerous drivers have even been filmed waving at cameras.

Case Study:
O. J. Simpson Car Chase

In 1994, football star O. J. Simpson was suspected of murdering his wife. When he failed to turn himself in to the Los Angeles Police Department, the police tracked him down to a white Ford Bronco being driven by a close friend. However, Simpson threatened to commit suicide. Instead of stopping the vehicle, the police followed it for more than two hours in a low-speed chase across Los Angeles.

The media soon picked up the story. By the time Simpson gave himself up, more than a dozen helicopters had filmed the chase—some networks even interrupted their usual broadcasts to bring audiences live coverage. Thousands of people lined bridges and overpasses to watch the Ford Bronco drive past. It is estimated that as many as 95 million viewers watched news footage of the event.

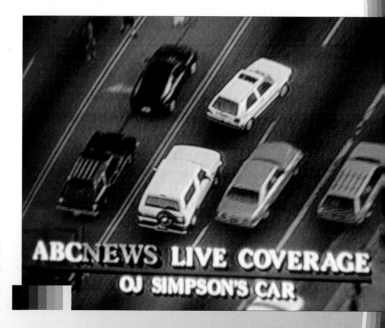

ABC's live broadcast tracked O. J. Simpson's white 4x4, which is shown in the middle of the picture.

Balanced Reporting

Most news organizations, such as CNN, the BBC, and the Australian Broadcasting Corporation, aim to report the facts and offer a balanced view of events. Audiences want to feel that they are getting the truth. But balanced reporting can be a difficult thing to achieve. What appears impartial to some may seem heavily biased to others.

Bias in the News

Many news organizations are privately owned. These organizations may be less concerned with impartiality. Their owners may have strong political views and seek to reach audiences who share their views. They may also try to influence public opinion by employing journalists and commentators who support their version and opinion of events, while giving fewer opportunities to those who oppose them.

Selective Reporting

This bias can be seen in the media's reporting of crime statistics. These

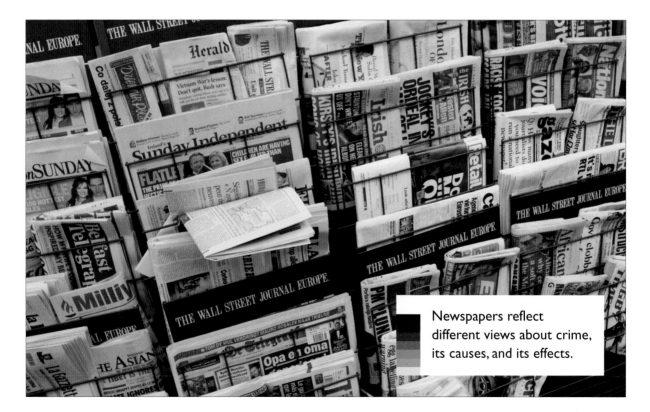

Newspapers reflect different views about crime, its causes, and its effects.

statistics come from a variety of sources and are often very detailed. A news outlet will often select a small sample. It may choose the figures that make the most exciting news story, or it may select only those statistics that support its view and the presumed view of its audience. For example, if a news organization supports the government, it may try to show that crime is falling—evidence that the government is doing a good job. If a news organization opposes the government, it may try to show that crime is increasing—evidence that the government's policies are failing.

Bias can also be seen in the types of crime highlighted by a particular newspaper or TV channel.

Rush Limbaugh makes no secret of his views and regularly ridicules liberal attitudes to crime on his show.

• Up for Discussion •

Some journalists only investigate and deliver the news, while others give their opinions and speculate about it. What responsibilities, if any, does a journalist or commentator have in the presentation of stories about crime?

Hidden Bias

Political bias is not a crime, but other types of bias spread hatred and are much less acceptable to most people. Xenophobia is a bias against or fear of minority groups such as homeless people or immigrants. Racial prejudice or fear may be concealed or exercised more subtly by the media, the police, or the general public.

During the riots in France in 2005, images such as this burning vehicle revealed what was happening. It also helped to spread fear among the general population.

Race and the Police

The police face a difficult task in avoiding claims of racial prejudice. They are required to be color blind—treating every person in the same way, regardless of race. However, they are sometimes accused of exercising discriminatory policies or allowing racist views. The accidental deaths of two teenagers of North African origin in Paris in 2005 were blamed by some on the fact that they were being chased by police who allegedly singled out young immigrants for harassment. Rioting in several French cities followed, fanned by media coverage.

Media Provocation

There are many ways in which the media can provoke or inflame existing prejudices. In a suburb of Sydney,

Australia, in 2005, tensions between local and immigrant youths, sparked by an alleged attack on two lifeguards, escalated after the circulation of anonymous text messages calling on the white population to attack those of Middle Eastern appearance. The growing violence attracted extensive media coverage that showed images of racist posters and slogans as the rioting gathered pace. After the events, radio talk show host Alan Jones was found to have breached the race code of the Australian Communications and Media Authority by broadcasting material likely to encourage violence against people of Middle Eastern origin.

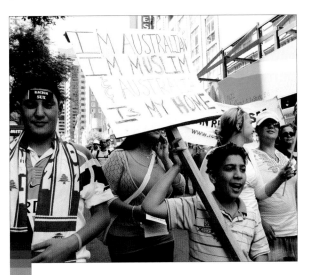

Antiracism protesters marched peacefully through Sydney, Australia, after the race riots of 2005.

Case Study: Riots in Los Angeles

In 1991, a speeding black motorist named Rodney King was stopped in Los Angeles and severely beaten by four white police officers. A member of the public taped the beating and this footage caused outrage around the world. The Los Angeles Police Department was accused of institutionalized racism. However, in 1992, the four officers were cleared of assault. Riots immediately broke out across the city. In the aftermath of the riots, some media outlets were accused of editing the video of the beating to leave out evidence that Rodney King was resisting arrest. Others were accused of sending out black journalists to report on the riots at the height of the violence, while relying on white commentators in the studio to pass judgment on events.

• Up for Discussion •

Why do you think that the video of Rodney King may have been edited by news organizations? What kind of edits do you think might have occurred? What effects might such editing have?

Glamorizing Crime

Books, films, and TV programs have a long history of making heroes out of criminals. Highwaymen, the Mafia, gangland—these worlds are made to seem exciting, risky, even romantic. Weapons are glamorized and criminals are shown "beating the system."

Criminals Become Celebrities

Serious crimes generate large amounts of media coverage. We see a criminal's face on the news, we become familiar with his or her story, and the criminal becomes famous. Sometimes this means they can build a career out of their newfound notoriety. Nick Leeson, a financial trader, caused the collapse of Barings Bank in Singapore in 1995 after defrauding the bank of $1.3 billion in order to cover up previous mistakes. He was sentenced to six and a half years in prison, but what he had done had made him famous. He wrote a book about his experiences, which was made into a film called *Rogue Trader*. Leeson's official web site now describes his "incredible life story" and how he has become "one of the world's most in-demand conference and after-dinner speakers."

Nick Leeson is escorted past the waiting media on his return to the UK after his prison sentence.

• Up for Discussion •

Why do you think some people see criminals as glamorous?

What criminals can you think of that the media has made into sympathetic, even romantic, figures?

Rap Music in the News

Rap music, garage, and hip-hop have often been accused of glorifying guns and violence. The work of artists such as Snoop Dogg and 50 Cent appears to condone petty gangsters, drugs, and the necessity of guns in their lyrics.

However, the artists and their promoters deny that there is a link between lyrics about violence and an increase in gun crime.

Case Study: 50 Cent

50 Cent is one of many successful U.S. rap artists whose lyrics reflect the violent reality of his life. 50 Cent was dealing drugs at 12, and in 2000, at 25, he was shot nine times at close range. He has also been stabbed and involved in several other violent disputes. A film about his life was criticized for glamorizing gun crime. He responded by pointing out that many films depicted weapons in their promotional material and that Get Rich or Die Tryin' was no different. The controversy ensured extra publicity for the film, but some people think he should not profit from his criminal background.

Artist 50 Cent's poster for his film *Get Rich or Die Tryin'* has caused controversy because it shows him with a gun and a baby.

Fiction or Real Life?

Crime sells. Sometimes it seems as if we can't get enough of it. Along with seeing all of the true crime in the news, we read crime novels, watch films and TV dramas about crime, or play video games in which we can actually "take part" in graphic scenes of violence. But is all this exposure to fictional crime affecting our attitudes toward real crime?

Cop Shows

TV shows about police officers, crimes, and procedures have always been popular. In recent years, hard-hitting dramas such as *The Wire* or shows such as *CSI* appear to present gritty, harsh reality to audiences who may know little about law enforcement in the real world. Many characters are either corrupt or mavericks working outside official procedures. These shows do not always show the painstaking, monotonous, and often boring nature of most police investigations. Some commentators suggest that they distort our view of the justice system, giving us false expectations or making us unduly cynical about law enforcement.

Violent Computer Games

Unlike TV, a viewer with video or computer games can actually participate in "virtual violence." Because of this type of participation and the potentially addictive nature of video games, they have been blamed for

Dixons, a UK retailer, removed *Manhunt* from its stores in 1994 after the parents of teenager Stefan Pakeerah blamed the violent video game for their son's murder.

Case Study: Murder at Columbine

On April 20, 1999, teenagers Eric Harris and Dylan Klebold went on an armed rampage at Columbine High School in Colorado. They killed 12 students and a teacher before shooting themselves. Investigations into the massacre revealed video tapes showing one of the killers with a sawn-off shotgun that he called Arlene— allegedly after a character in the computer game Doom. The families of the Columbine victims tried to sue 25 companies who made similar computer games, arguing that they were partly to blame for turning vulnerable children into "monster killers." The case was dismissed.

Teenagers Eric Harris and Dylan Klebold were caught on CCTV as they stalked their victims in Columbine High School.

encouraging aggressive behavior in some users. In 1994, British 14-year-old Stefan Pakeerah was brutally murdered by a 17-year-old friend after the boys had been playing the adult video game *Manhunt*, in which players score points for violent killings. Stefan's parents and several newspapers blamed the game but no link was ever proved. The police concluded that the motive most likely was robbery.

• *Up for Discussion* •

Many people enjoy playing violent video games. Do you think there is any truth in the view that violent video games influence some people to copy such behavior in real life? Why?

The Media
Stunt

Campaigners are always seeking publicity for their causes. So some campaigners try to attract attention by staging an event or stunt that the media will find impossible to resist. Sometimes these stunts break the law. But campaigners know that getting arrested is a great way to get their views into the news.

Case Study: Plane Stupid

The UK campaign group Plane Stupid has carried out a number of media stunts that have caused widespread disruption and achieved substantial publicity for their cause. Plane Stupid's goals are simple: to further the struggle against airport expansion and greenhouse gas emissions from aviation. In pursuit of their goals, they have occupied a number of airport runways, frequently obstructing airplane departures. In 2008, they climbed onto the roof of the British Houses of Parliament, draped banners, and chained themselves to the building. On each occasion, the media have documented their actions.

Workmen repair a fence at Stansted Airport in the United Kingdom in 2008 after protesters from Plane Stupid broke in and occupied a runway.

Under what circumstances, if any, do you think that campaigners who resort to illegal stunts are justified in their actions? Plane Stupid has been given extra publicity in this book by the very fact that their name has been mentioned. Do you think this is acceptable?

Into the Picture

Some media stunts are all about getting the right photograph. So the stunt has to be visually exciting or even shocking. Animal rights activists threw a bag of flour over actress Lindsay Lohan outside a nightclub in 2008 because she was wearing fur. Her celebrity status meant that cameras were clicking and the pictures appeared in precisely the types of magazines and online sites that the campaigners hoped to target.

Spot the Campaigner

Other activists pull high-profile stunts to place themselves in the public eye. This includes scaling public buildings in superhero outfits (Fathers4Justice) or chaining themselves to equipment used to export coal from Australia (Young People Fight Against Climate Change). Such stunts tend to involve illegal trespassing and often end in arrests, but charges are often dropped before the case reaches court.

Actress Lindsay Lohan has attracted the attention of animal rights activists for wearing fur to high profile events, such as film premieres.

Name
and Shame

When people are found guilty of a crime, they are punished. They may be fined, ordered to do community service, or sent to prison. But have they learned their lesson? Is there any danger that they might commit a crime again? The media may publish an offender's name, photograph, and address with details of the crime so that people are made aware of what the offender has done. They are "named and shamed."

A Community's Right?

Of course, anyone can learn the name of an offender by examining court records or by reading media reports of a case. But naming and shaming is a deliberate attempt to prevent the offender from disappearing into the background. For example, some people feel they have the right to know if a sex offender with multiple convictions has moved into their area. They want to be able to protect themselves and their children. However, such information has, at times, led to vigilante attacks against individuals who have already been punished for their crimes.

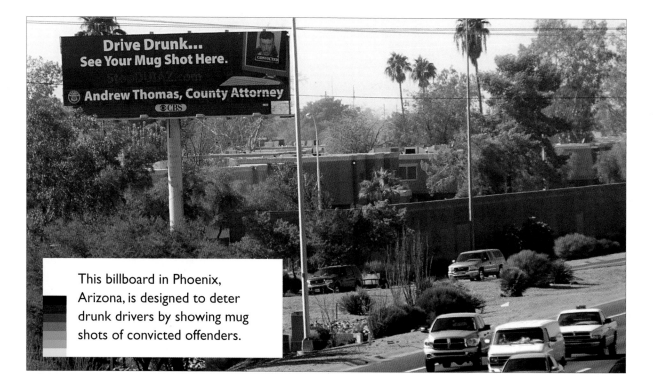

This billboard in Phoenix, Arizona, is designed to deter drunk drivers by showing mug shots of convicted offenders.

Case Study: A Controversial Campaign

In 2000, an eight-year-old British girl, Sarah Payne, was assaulted and murdered by a convicted sex offender. The United Kingdom has no system to alert parents about sex offenders living in their area, unlike Megan's Law in the United States. The News of the World *newspaper began a campaign to name and shame every convicted sex offender in the country by publishing photographs and information about them. The campaign was controversial and not supported by most child protection groups, who felt that it would merely push convicted offenders into hiding. Also, several innocent men were attacked in cases of mistaken identity. The* News of the World *eventually dropped its campaign.*

• *Up for Discussion* •

Some people argue that the public have a right to know about convicted criminals in their area. Others argue that these offenders have done their time and now have a right to privacy. What's your view?

Young Offenders

It isn't just sex offenders, violent criminals, or drunk drivers who are targeted by naming and shaming. In the United Kingdom, for example, young offenders who are subject to an Anti-social Behaviour Order (ASBO) may find their details in the news. One newspaper ran a campaign with a hotline for people to provide information about local troublemakers. However, children's rights campaigners have expressed concern about targeting young offenders in this way.

After the murder of UK schoolgirl Sarah Payne, the *News of the World* newspaper asked readers to support its campaign to name and shame convicted sex offenders.

Trial by Media

When a serious crime is committed, the media takes advantage of the public's desire for information by offering 24-hour coverage of the story as it unfolds. The crime is examined from every angle. Journalists speculate about what happened and why. They ask the questions they think the public is asking. This demand can lead to "trial by media," where the media passes judgment before a trial is concluded in a court.

Collecting evidence needs to be carried out slowly and meticulously.

A Quick Result

Using the media to keep the public informed has many advantages during a police investigation. The police can appeal for witnesses, alert people to any danger, and show that they are following the appropriate procedures. However, detective work can be laborious and time-consuming. The media wants fresh information on a daily or even hourly basis. Journalists may become impatient. They soon start to speculate or question the ability of the police to do their job. In the highly charged atmosphere that follows a crime such as murder, the police are often under pressure to obtain a quick result.

• Up for Discussion •

Some people argue that the media is simply doing its job when it speculates about a crime before anyone is convicted.
What do you think?

Case Study: O.J. Simpson Murder Trial

In 1995, football star O. J. Simpson was brought to trial for the murder of his wife and her friend. The case had attracted intense media coverage in the months leading up to the trial. Lawyers were concerned that it would be impossible to find an impartial jury—one that had not been influenced by speculation in the media.

A jury was eventually chosen and the trial that followed was one of the most publicized in history. TV cameras filmed events inside the courtroom. Polls were broadcast on whether or not members of the public thought O. J. Simpson was guilty. In the end, he was acquitted, but media speculation about the murders and the trial continues to this day.

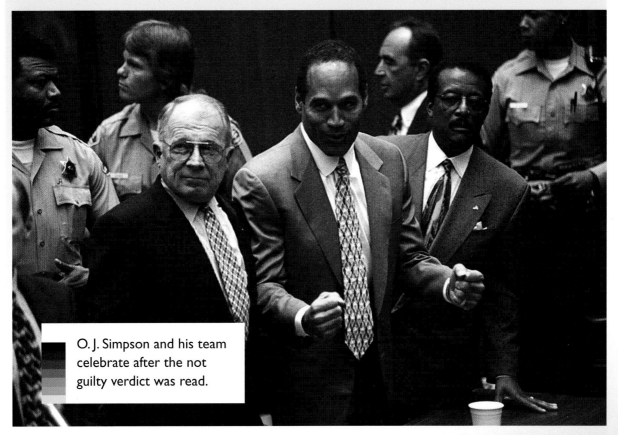

O. J. Simpson and his team celebrate after the not guilty verdict was read.

Flawed Evidence

It took three separate trials to convict two brothers of the manslaughter of eleven-year-old Damilola Taylor in London in 2000. The forensic evidence presented by the police at the first two trials was seriously flawed. Critics suggested that forensics teams had been under pressure from the media to find evidence and make arrests. However, significant information leaked to the media also damaged the evidence of key witnesses.

A Cause of Crime?

Sometimes the media may appear to tempt people into crime. Usually, this is the last thing that editors and journalists intend when they broadcast information or offer a reward. However, by publicizing how a crime is committed or how a witness may stand to benefit, they may provide the motivation or the means to carry out some crimes.

Copycat Crime

Some TV programs such as *The Real Hustle* specialize in demonstrating how crimes such as fraud or burglary are carried out. Their stated aim is to help members of the public to protect themselves against such crimes. By exposing a con man's technique, for example, audiences can learn how to avoid falling for their scams. But the scams set up by the show hosts are generally so entertaining, convincing, and successful that some critics have suggested they actually teach people how to con innocent people.

The Real Hustle hosts Paul Wilson, Jessica-Jane Clement, and Alexis Conran at an awards ceremony.

• Up for Discussion •

Karen Matthews kidnapped her own daughter because of the prospect of a newspaper reward. Does the media share any responsibility for the crime?

In February 2008, nine-year-old Shannon Matthews disappeared on her way home from school in Dewsbury in the UK. A police investigation began, but some critics accused the media of failing to give her disappearance the same coverage afforded to more well-off families such as the McCanns, whose daughter Madeleine had disappeared in May 2007 while on vacation with her parents in Portugal. Critics maintained that Shannon's story was given less media coverage because she came from a single-parent family in a deprived area of Britain. However, a reward for information was eventually offered by the Sun newspaper.

Shannon was found 24 days later, drugged and hidden away at an apartment belonging to Michael Donovan, a relative of her mother's boyfriend. However, in the weeks after Shannon's rescue, more details emerged.

Supporters gather to search for missing schoolgirl Shannon Matthews in her hometown of Dewsbury in 2008.

Shannon's mother, Karen, had conspired with Michael Donovan to kidnap her daughter with the intention of "finding" her in a public place and claiming the reward. Karen was aware of the fund established to help find Madeleine McCann and hoped to benefit from some of this money. Karen Matthews and Michael Donovan were tried and later imprisoned.

Graham Dudman, managing editor of the Sun newspaper, said: "We will pay big money for the right story and other papers do as well and that's part of a free press ... but we don't offer a reward without the complete blessing of the police."

Checkbook Journalism

Journalists don't just rely on press conferences and court reports for information about a crime. They carry out their own investigations. But journalists don't have to follow strict police procedures. They may pay a witness for an interview or a piece of information. Some people argue that this "checkbook journalism" is open to abuse.

Exaggerating Evidence

One of the problems with paying witnesses is that they may be tempted to exaggerate their claims to make their story more exciting and more valuable to the media. Witnesses might also withhold evidence until they know they will be paid. They may even make up stories, as with the case of Karen Matthews who kidnapped her own daughter in the hope of getting a reward.

The Power of Money

Some types of checkbook journalism are more open to manipulation than others. For example, a journalist might offer money to a witness to tell his or her story, but only if the case ends in the conviction of the accused. The witness might decide to withhold evidence that casts doubt on a guilty verdict. Others may offer bribes to journalists to tell a story in a certain way or not publish it at all.

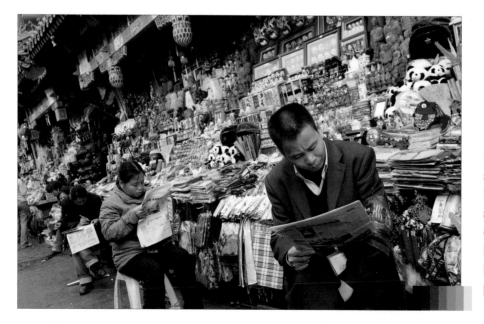

China's media has been accused of accepting bribes from businesses and government officials who want to halt any investigation into failure or poor performance.

Case Study: The Beckham "Kidnap" Case

In 2002, a British newspaper uncovered a plot to kidnap Victoria Beckham, former pop star and wife of soccer player David Beckham. But the trial of the alleged plotters collapsed the following year when the court heard how the News of the World had paid about $14,000 to a convicted criminal to tell his version of events. The newspaper argued that it had uncovered the plot after a legitimate investigation and no information was withheld from the police. However, the judge decided that the witness's evidence was unreliable because he had been paid for it. It is not illegal for journalists in the United Kingdom to pay witnesses for their stories, but the issue remains controversial and many media organizations have now agreed to a voluntary ban.

David and Victoria Beckham with their children in 2009. The Beckhams have to be aware of their security at all times and employ a number of bodyguards.

• Up for Discussion •

Some people argue that payments to witnesses are sometimes the only way to obtain information on a crime. Perhaps some witnesses deserve financial compensation for their bravery in coming forward. What do you think?

Under Surveillance

Cameras are everywhere. CCTV cameras watch us in public spaces and can be a tool in crime prevention. Cell phone cameras mean that we can take pictures or make videos whenever we like. These images are increasingly used as evidence when a crime is committed. But some think that this surveillance intrudes into our private lives.

CCTV and Crime

The success of CCTV in crime prevention and detection depends on cameras working properly. The UK has more security cameras than any other country in Europe. Yet in 2008, the British police warned that only 3 percent of street robberies in London were solved using CCTV images. They pointed out that there was no fear of CCTV because people assume the cameras aren't working or

• Up for Discussion •

Does the presence of CCTV make you feel safer? Some people feel that its intrusion into ordinary people's lives is too great a price to pay. What's your view?

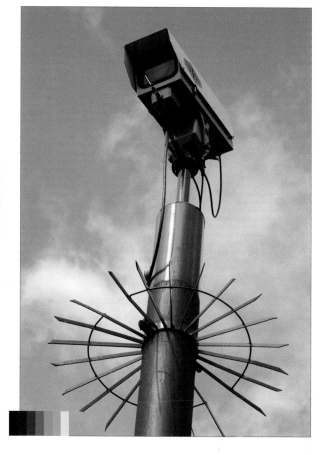

CCTV is often seen as a tool in the prevention of crime—thieves may not risk being caught on camera.

that they aren't positioned correctly. However, CCTV has also been used to track the movements of criminals or witnesses in a number of high-profile crimes such as the Columbine shootings. The images don't prevent the crimes taking place, but they can show what happened and who was involved.

Onto the Internet

Images may provide evidence of crimes, but sometimes the presence of cameras can motivate people to commit crime. Cameras on cell phones have led to instances where someone is assaulted and the incident is filmed and shared on the Internet. There also are issues about the way CCTV footage is monitored and who has access to it. For instance, should CCTV images of suspects be placed on the Internet by the police before a court has found them innocent or guilty?

Case Study: The Shooting of Jean Charles de Menezes

On July 7, 2005, four suicide bombers detonated devices on the subway in London, killing 52 people and injuring more than 700. The police recovered 6,000 hours of CCTV footage that provided evidence about the bombers and their movements. A second bomb plot was foiled on July 21, 2005. The following day, London police shot and killed Jean Charles de Menezes, believing he was one of the failed bombers. But they had made a terrible mistake. Jean Charles de Menezes was innocent.

Police surveillance had completely failed to establish Jean Charles de Menezes's identity. However, CCTV footage shown at his inquest helped to establish the truth about what

CCTV images show Jean Charles de Menezes (JC) as he walked through a London underground station just before he was shot and killed in July 2005.

happened. The cameras provided vital evidence that he had not acted suspiciously or jumped over a ticket barrier as the police had claimed.

Crime Online

In recent years, the Internet has become a focus for many types of crime. The nature of this media means that information can be exchanged, infiltrated, manipulated, and downloaded around the world at the press of a button. Crimes such as hacking, identity theft, and fraud can cross national borders and become very difficult to trace. The police and other law enforcement agencies are struggling to catch up.

Case Study: Cyber Attack

In 2007, broadcasters and government departments in Estonia were bombarded by electronic requests for information, which overwhelmed their computer servers and caused many systems to crash. The incident was seen as a deliberate attack on the country's infrastructure that appeared to originate from Russia. Media headlines spoke of a cyber war, but the involvement of Russian officials has never been proved and only one person has been convicted of a crime as a result of the attacks. However, the incident has highlighted the vulnerability of electronic data and the need for international cooperation in protecting it from criminals and terrorists.

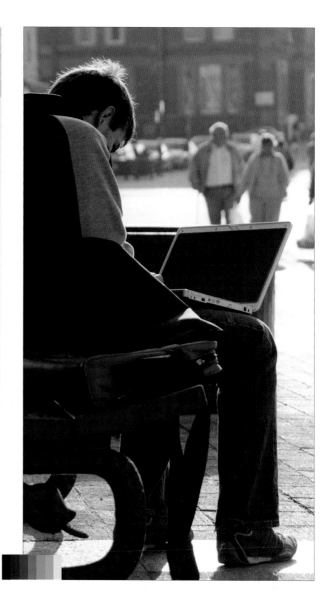

A few basic precautions, such as installing a firewall and other software, can help someone avoid becoming a victim of crime online.

Access All Areas?

Most of us want to limit access to private details such as bank statements, e-mails, browsing history, and Facebook profiles for reasons of security or privacy. But all of this data is useful to criminals who want to infiltrate aspects of our lives. Pedophiles and sex offenders use false identities to approach children online. Information such as a home address and who lives there can be used by burglars or identity thieves.

The Internet is like a public announcement system. Policing it is difficult, and users need to take care over the kinds of data they place there.

Phishing

Phishing is a type of deception carried out online. In one type of fraud, people receive unsolicited e-mails asking for bank details and security codes. The e-mails are often made to appear like official requests from banks or the government. When victims reply, the data is used to steal money from their online accounts. It is important to remember that a real bank would never ask for such details online. However, installing anti-spyware software can help to block phishing e-mails.

• Up for Discussion •

In most countries, the law is changing to allow law enforcement agencies access to private e-mails, Facebook accounts, and text messages. They argue that this is vital for catching criminals. Others argue that this is an invasion of privacy and may be open to abuse. What do you think?

Power and Influence

The media wields immense power to spread information and influence public opinion. This includes our views on crime and our fears about it. However, the media has no power without an audience. Its response to crime is influenced by what we—the public—want.

What Do People Want?

A 2008 survey by the New South Wales Bureau of Crime Statistics in Australia found that most people vastly overestimated the number of violent crimes committed and underestimated conviction rates for assault and home burglary. Some experts have concluded that the media is to blame for presenting a distorted picture of crime and the ability of the police and courts to deal with it. After all, crimes such as insurance fraud or benefit fraud and stories about low crime rates aren't very exciting. But is the media merely responding to a public interest in stories about violent crime?

Into the Future

As the Internet and digital media grow, traditional newspapers appear to be in decline. Some people fear that this means the end of proper investigative reporting where journalists are able to

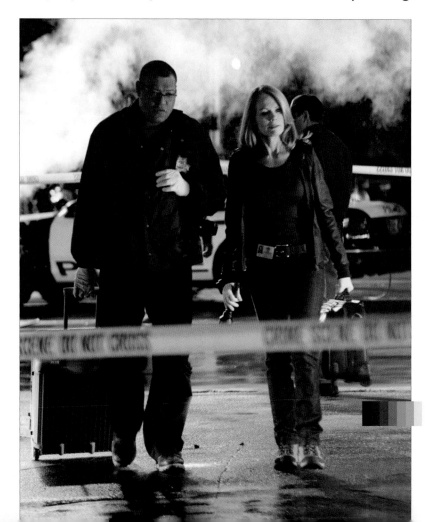

Crime dramas such as *CSI* are popular, but do they provide a realistic assessment of the most common types of crime?

• Up for Discussion •

Some people think the media abuses its power, distorting our views about crime. Other people think that the media simply reflects the public interest. What issues in this book have been of most concern to you?

spend weeks or even months digging out facts and interviewing witnesses to establish an independent perspective. Picture-led TV news is still a major force, though our demand for 24-hour coverage can dilute some of its power. While the Internet can appear to distort crime coverage and focus on the more sensational stories, there are other signs that it can be a useful tool in spreading information about crime, particularly at a local level.

You can have your say on the media by becoming part of it. Set up a blog, write for an online newspaper, or post a report on a video-sharing web site in response to crime stories in your area.

Case Study: Making it Local

Crime mapping is a recent innovation that combines web-based maps with local crime statistics to provide information about crime in different neighborhoods. Sites such as www.everyblock.com are increasingly able to provide a crime map not only of individual U.S. cities, but specific streets and blocks. Such innovations are already making an appearance in other countries including the United Kingdom, where local government and police are seeking to establish stronger connections between the public and the justice system.

David Cameron, the UK Conservative Party leader, demonstrates crime mapping in London.

London ward, April 2008: burglary, robbery & vehicle crime

Glossary

acquitted Found not guilty of a crime.

biased Weighted in favor of one side over another.

capital punishment The death penalty; sentenced to death.

car jacking Holding up a vehicle and stealing it, often after threatening the driver.

CCTV Closed circuit television, used for security.

con Deceiving or tricking someone for financial gain.

crime mapping A map showing the type, location, and number of crimes in a particular area.

crime wave A noticeable increase in a particular type of crime.

deter To try to prevent something, such as a crime, from taking place.

discriminatory Putting someone at an unfair disadvantage on the basis of race, religion, gender, or age.

documentaries Factual, investigative TV programs or films.

editing Piecing together or making cuts to different elements of a written report or film footage.

fictional Made up; not true.

firewall Software used to protect a computer against hackers and unwelcome intrusions.

forensic evidence Physical evidence, such as blood or cloth fiber, that can be tested by scientists and used in a trial.

fraud Deception, often for financial gain.

hacking Using computer technology to gain access to someone else's private information.

identity theft Illegal use of someone else's personal details such as name and address.

impartial Balanced; fair; without bias.

inquest An inquiry into the circumstances of someone's death.

institutionalized racism Where the policies and procedures of an organization such as the police are prejudiced against certain ethnic groups.

maverick Someone who breaks the rules or goes against the popular view.

name and shame Publishing photos, names, and other personal details about people who have broken the law.

news blackout A decision not to publish or broadcast a particular news item, often for reasons of safety or security.

phishing Sending unsolicited e-mails disguised as official requests for information such as bank details in order to steal money.

prejudice Fear or dislike of a particular group of people on the basis of race, sexuality, background, religion, or nationality.

press conference Delivering an announcement to a group of journalists; answering journalists' questions.

producer a person who supervises or finances a program.

ratings Audience figures; number of people watching or listening to a broadcast.

reenactment A reconstruction of a crime with actors taking the roles of victims, witnesses, and criminals.

speculate Make a guess on the basis of limited evidence.

statistics Numbers; percentages.

stereotype A cliché; a limited view of someone.

stunt An event or action designed to gain maximum attention.

surveillance Watching, for example via CCTV.

talk radio A type of radio show where audience members phone in and debate topical issues with presenters and their guests.

terrorist Someone who seeks to spread fear and panic through violence or who uses violence to gain publicity for a cause.

vandalism Illegal damage to property.

vigilante Someone who takes the law into his or her own hands.

witness Someone who is present during a crime and can give evidence about what happened to the police and the courts.

xenophobia Fear of strangers or foreigners.

Further Information

Books

Issues Today: Crime by Lisa Firth (Independence Educational Publishers, 2008)

Voices: Violence on the Screen by Clive Gifford (Smart Apple Media, 2007)

What's Your View? Dealing with Crime by Judith Anderson (Smart Apple Media, 2006)

Web Sites

http://www.disastercenter.com/crime
U. S. crime statistics from 1960 to 2008 by state and type of crime.

http://www.npr.org/templates/story/story.php?storyId=91883044&ft=1&f=1020
This site discusses the difficult relationship between the FBI and the media.

http://www.amw.com/about_amw/index.cfm
This is the official site of *America's Most Wanted* television show. Host John Walsh presents new cases every week so concerned citizens can help track America's most wanted fugitives.

http://www.pbs.org/newshour/bb/media/jan-june00/standoff_3-29.html
A discussion on how reporters should relate to police when covering volatile situations.

http://www.pbs.org/newshour/bb/media/jan-june99/rtda_4-29.html
Following the Columbine school shootings, "Guidelines for Covering Hostage-Taking Crises, Police Raids, Prison Uprisings or Terrorist Actions" were issued to media outlets across the nation.

http://www.tiporangecounty.org/Resources/Dealing%20With%20the%20Media.pdf
This site presents the victim's rights when dealing with the media.

http://www.publiceye.org/defendingjustice/overview/beckett_media.html
This site discusses crime in the news.

Note to parents and teachers: Every effort has been made by the publishers to ensure that these web sites are suitable for children, are of the highest educational value, and contain no inappropriate or offensive material. However, because of the nature of the Internet, it is impossible to guarantee that the contents of these sites will not be altered. We strongly advise that Internet access be supervised by a responsible adult.

Index

Explore the other titles in the *Media Power* series.